Transcending Greatness

The Lawrence Perkins Story

To My TRue fAMily Mrs Shayonte Gilmore I Love You AlwAys STAy focused !

By
Lawrence Perkins

Heart Thoughts Publishing
Floyds Knobs, Indiana

Lawrence Perkins
Lawrenceperkins@sbcglobal.net
www.LawrencePerkins.com
773-759-8720

Heart Thoughts Publishing
P.O. Box 536
Floyds Knobs, IN 47119
www.VanessaCollinsOnline.com
Vancollins@aol.com

Printed in the United States of America

First Printing, 2011

ISBN-13: 978-0-9823325-2-8
ISBN-10: 0-9823325-2-1
LCCN: 2011921570

Heart Thoughts Publishing
2015 Leanders Rd
Floyds Knobs, IN 47119

Dedication

To my mother, Mary Perkins who never gave up on me and my father Lawrence Perkins Sr. (Deceased) who raised nine children and two of his own. He taught me the power of being a provider. To my sons Dorian and Lawrence Perkin who I hope will be inspired by this book to achieve greatness. To my brothers and sisters.

To my teachers Dr. Odis Richardson, a mentor, father, teacher, social worker, counselor and a true FRIEND; Dr. Hamberlin who told me I can be whatever I want to be and taught me how to conduct myself as young man and respect my community; Dr. Larry Thomas who gave me a chance to test the waters as a substitute teacher; Mr. Rangel CEO UNO Charter School Network who believed in me and gave me a chance to go to New Orleans to make a difference in the heart of a devastated area.

To Mrs. Oden, Mrs. Garner Stewart, Ms. Valoree Harrington, Mrs. Ethel Southern, and Dr. Grace Dawson who gave me a chance to come back to my former school Beethoven where I attended for nine years to teach and reach out to others.

Special thanks to Mr. Smith, the Director of the Lunchroom at Alcorn State University who allowed me to eat when I wasn't even enrolled in school; Mr. Powell, the Director of Students of the Dormitory at Alcorn State University who allowed me to live in the dorms without being a student. Special thanks to Mr. Louis Ingram.

Special thanks to Operation Push, Rev. Jessie Jackson Sr. and Mrs. Ora Sanders for the $1000 scholarship to go to college and the Operation Push Free Food Basket when we were in need of food to eat.

Special thanks to my Spiritual Awakening Church Family, Pastor Herbert, Mary Agee, Pastor Hughes, Pastor Yvette Bruce, and Mrs. Jean Cotton Philip who encouraged me to attend college.

Special thanks to my Bread of Life Church family, Pastor Leon Johnson, Mrs. Jackie Ward, Mr. Burns, and Mrs. Glenda Ellison.

Special thanks to my Greater St. John Bible Church family, Sr. Pastor Ira J. Acree, Pastor Bernard Lilly; my GSJ Drill Team, Children Church, Mrs. Deola Gaiter, Ms. Felicia Tims; and Ms. Betty Bady for assisting with the preparation of this book.

I thank God for Bardell Wilson, Tyrone Cotton and the Cotton boys, Mr. Darryl Battie, Men of Purpose, Mr. Eric David, Mr. Gallardo, Ms. Nicole Christian, Ms. Sabrina Hawthorn, Mr. Thomas Kendrick (DJ Slugo) and DuSable High School Class of `87. A special thanks to Mrs. Renee Brown who kept the class together.

Special thanks to CEO Paul Vallas in New Orleans, Ms. Woods, and Hope Kyle Mitchell for their encouragement.

Special thanks to my cousins Ms. Nekida Harden (ACN), Ms. Sherice Shana Perkins, Ms. Carlean, and Mr. Ralpheal, who helped start New Anointed Ministry.

I would like to also thank my Redeeming World Church Family, Pastor Paul A. Southerland, Bishop Kevin Chambers, Rev. Arlene Bell and Rev. Vanessa Collins. Special thanks to my aunt Rev. Georgia Sanders for inviting me to Redeeming Ministry.

This book is also dedicated to two of my former 8th grade students, Robert Owens and Devon Harris. They were from the Back of the Yards community and they died much too young.

Table of Contents

Foreword

The very first time I saw Lawrence, he was breaking a school rule along with his friends who called him 'Fella.' It was obvious that Lawrence was the leader and he made no bones about trying to talk his way out of a suspension or a punishment for being late to class and hanging out in the washroom. I was on hall duty that day, a teacher's nightmare at DuSable High School on Chicago's South side. Every morning a group of male students gathered in the boy's washroom on the third floor near my post. They were loud, disorderly, and sometimes left the washroom smelling like reefers. There were times when they left cigarettes butts. Once I found a Canadian Mist bottle on the floor. I was a determined young teacher in those days, and eager to stop these infractions and to have the culprits suspended from school for a few days.

On the day I met Lawrence, I enlisted the help of a veteran teacher, Dr. Emiel Hamberlin. Every student in that school feared Doc's wrath, and respected even the sound of his voice. Doc blocked one side of the washroom, and I covered the other. Now, I had these villains blocked in, and I shouted out in my sternest voice, "Dr. Hamberlin, come in through that door and I'll get this one." Well about ten of those guys rushed through my door, and I was only able to stop the last two or three. Lawrence was caught! "Young man," I screamed, "Why aren't you guys in class?" The others stood quiet while Lawrence began to give reason after reason why they were in the washroom after the bell had sounded. "You're going to be suspended today", I screeched. "We're going to the principal's office right now." With that look, which I came to call "the good fella look," he started to plead his case. "Mr. Richardson if you take me to the principal they are going to put me out of this school! Don't you want to see a black boy get his education?" "Please Mr. Richardson give us a break." I was not in a break-giving mood. Lawrence just kept on talking and pleading and giving excuses for being late and in the washroom. Then I perked up thinking, this guy is pretty articulate and maybe he would be a good candidate for my debate team. With Dr. Hamberlin as a witness, I got the three of them to agree to participate in my debate team class after school, with the promise that if they missed one day I would take them to the principal's office.

When I look back, it's with pride, because as I ponder on those days, I realize it is all history now. Lawrence and his friends Bardell and David became some of my best debaters. Lawrence even became the President of the

DuSable Debate Society in his senior year. He had no idea of the skill he had, and the power it gave him when used in positive ways. I worked with those young men until they lost interest in all of the other foolishnesses in which they were involved.

It was the beginning of a new Lawrence. His attitude began to change. Lawrence began to believe that he could achieve greatness. He aspired to higher goals, including running for senior class president. In his best debater's style "the good fella look," he made me pledge to help him. We got together and made plans for his campaign.

I can still remember our first meeting. It was at his home in the Robert Taylor Housing Projects. I had asked my church pastor, Rev. Dr. Bobby O. McCarroll to join me since it was not always safe to be in the projects on Saturdays. Rev. McCarroll and I entered the apartment and sat with Lawrence around the kitchen table. The meeting was productive. We advised Lawrence to select five male students to run as a team. For the past ten years not one male student had served as class president. We told him to develop a campaign slogan and to bring the candidates by my office as soon as he got them together. He quickly assembled his team. He introduced his team and said that they had decided the slogan would be, "The Winning Team."

They came together, they campaigned, they excited the student-body, they inspired their classmates, they awed the teachers, and they won!

As I look back I can remember the excitement of those days. Five black young men running for officers of their graduating class. Five young black men who had come through tremendous adversities and obstacles were now certified leaders and as their teacher and mentor they made me proud.

Somewhere in the annals of DuSable history they will recall these young men and the affect they had on their class and on the entire school. They wanted to mentor the new freshmen students, plan school dances, parties, trips, and other activities. Recently, I attended one of their reunions (Class of 87) and I know that what his teachers and the school were doing in those days paid off with tremendous rewards. Lawrence was a school administrator, Bardell was a middle school teacher, Scott was successful in tele-communications, and Telkia was doing well in his business and dreaming of becoming a teacher. They were now responsible family men and their classmates matched their success in extraordinary numbers. Looking back, I can still feel the tears in my eyes on that day in the park, and the joy in my laughter just thinking that we had beaten the odds.

As a teacher, I believe that Lawrence Perkins' strongest characteristic is diligence. In every action he takes, he is diligent to stick with it until he achieves success or becomes the best that he can be. If you could have seen him during a debate round speaking so confidently, and searching for more powerful evidence, and struggling against foes that were far more privileged that he, you would have known then as I did that he would be a preacher or a teacher and definitely a leader. Lawrence's diligence is what his peers saw and why they followed him. Diligence is what made him face the challenge of college when the world had told him that black boys from the Robert Taylor Homes don't go to college. Even when his parents were so burdened with the tribulations of their lives he continued to head toward the light. I watched Lawrence, and mentored him as he grew into a wise young man and into a man that was willing to undertake difficult challenges that faced him. When he went to New Orleans to open a new school after the terrible Katrina Storm and Flood, it didn't matter to him the challenges, the obstacles, the burdens, the New Orleans culture, or the expectations of failure by those around him.

There is still so much more that I could say about Lawrence Perkins, but I was just his teacher, and what influence could I have had? The Glory belongs to God!

Odis Gene Richardson

Teacher, administrator, counselor, student activities coordinator, debate coach, chess coach, cheerleader coach, class sponsor, staff development coordinator, Union QUEST Presenter, Proposal Writing Consultant, Fellow with The Golden Apple Foundation, and community activist.

I recall my first encounter with Lawrence prior to becoming his English teacher at DuSable High School. I first met him when he was a very young boy in grammar school. I taught his older sisters: Renee and Sharon at Wendell Phillips High School. I had the opportunity to meet his entire family and I noticed those "piercing eyes" of his that looked straight through things that he did not know or was unfamiliar with.

Some years later after I had left Phillips and taught at Mather High School a few years, I suddenly found myself in room 204 at DuSable replacing Mrs. Connie Montgomery who had become an assistant principal. I noticed in my American Literature class a young man with those "same piercing eyes" from an earlier experience. I inquired and found out that Lawrence was the brother of my former students and our paths had again crossed.

The first thing that I noticed about Lawrence's greatness was that he did not like mediocrity. I had graded an assignment in which he had received a "C". He resubmitted it and I asked why? Lawrence replied, "I want an "A". I was stunned and shocked because in the urban culture of inner city schools, most students accepted a "C" with gladness. At this point I knew that Lawrence would transcend to something great.

I continued to watch his educational aspirations and he often told me that he would one day like to teach or preach. I continued to support all of his endeavors and assisted whenever needed to help ensure that he succeeded as a positive contributor to our society.

It was at DuSable that I began to network with Dr. Emiel Hamberlin, Mr. Odis Richardson, Mr. Fulton Nolen, and Ms. Sarah Dickens to provide Lawrence with financial and spiritual support to keep him in school until he matriculated from college.

Lawrence has always been a prolific speaker and had the profound ability to captivate and mesmerize his audience with thought-provoking ideas. He has the innate ability to inspire and motivate others to think outside the box and reach high for their dreams and aspirations.

One of my proudest moments was the day that Lawrence walked into Edward Coles Language Academy with his transcript from Alcorn State University. I was able to hire him as a substitute teacher for the Chicago Public

Schools and further recommended him to the late Dr. James Norris, Principal of Park Manor School as his Dean of students. Lawrence made me so proud and Dr. Norris never regretted having hired him. I will always love, respect, support and acknowledge Lawrence's Greatness!

Larry J. Thomas, Ed.D.

Former High School English Teacher, Principal Emeritus, Edward Coles Language Academy and South Shore High School

"A Man with Dedication" - Lawrence Perkins

Lawrence's trials and tribulations as a child in the inner-city molded him into an individual of outstanding growth and development. As a student of mine, Lawrence was the epitome of the adage: "What you can be is better than what you've been". I realized that Lawrence kept the faith of believing he could accomplish anything. What tremendous perseverance! He truly knows the POWER of FAITH.

As an educator and administrator, Lawrence Perkins displays enthusiasm and calmness in the most difficult situations. Time after time, he finds a way to excel under unacceptable conditions. He is indeed the definition of a certified problem-solver. Furthermore, Lawrence believes that each student can learn regardless of any learning disability. He expects that each student CAN learn ANYTHING; and he is not satisfied until that goal has been accomplished.

Lawrence Perkins not only teaches from the MIND but also from the HEART. Thus teaching is more than an intellectual exercise. The true beauty of Lawrence's teaching style is that he strives to improve a child's self-image, therefore building a child's character and self-esteem. With that being said, every student of his realizes how unique and special they are. These students go forward with a leadership mentality that will help them achieve their goals. It has been a delightful pleasure seeing Lawrence transcend greatness.

Cheers!
Dr. Emiel Hamberlin

Biology and horticulture teacher at DuSable High School, Inductee - National Teachers' Hall of Fame; Golden Apple Award Recipient, Newsweek Magazine, Inc., 100 American Heroes, State of Illinois Master Teacher Award Recipient, Outstanding Secondary Educator of America

Greatness is not measured by what a man or woman accomplishes, but by the opposition he or she has overcome to reach his goals.

Dorothy Height

Chapter 1

Not again, I thought to myself. The elevators were not working. The elevators were never working. But that's nothing new. It's expected when you live in the Robert Taylor Homes in Chicago. Things just don't work all of the time, most of the time. It comes with the territory.

Taking the stairs to the 4th floor was no picnic but I had done it before a number of times. My buddies and I would make a game out of it. But that day I decided to take a few hours away from the friends and the gang members. I never traveled by myself anymore, especially since joining the gang. It just wasn't safe. You never knew who you would run into.

As I opened the door and entered the stairway, the familiar aroma of mildew and urine invaded my nostrils. Going up the stairs, I noticed someone standing behind the door. In the dimness of the stairwell I could see that it was a young man, but no one that I had ever met before.

"Do you know who I am", the stranger asked. "No", I replied. "Who are you"?

"I'm the brother of the boy you jumped on a few weeks ago", he said.

A wave of anxiety hit me immediately. *I can talk my way out of this. I can always talk my way out of anything.* Being the youngest of 11 children taught me many things, especially how to get out of tight situations. I guess you would consider me a smooth talker. Although I grew up having speech issues, that never hampered my ability to talk my way out of things. In fact, it often helped the situation. It made me a little more adorable. It gave me the sympathy factor.

"Listen, I was not the only one that jumped on your brother. Why are you up in my face? He didn't die. That was a few weeks ago. It's over now", I said as I backed up toward the stairs. This was just a big misunderstanding.

It wasn't working this time. He didn't want to hear it. As we made eye contact, the anxiety in my stomach got worse. I could see it in his eyes, a look of evil, confident determination. I recognized that look and understood the feeling behind it. He was confident. He had a plan. He knew what he was going to do and he could not conceive of anyone stopping him. I remembered that feeling from when we jumped on his brother.

"We are going to kill you today", he said with the calmness of an assassin.

I gotta get out of here. My only hope was to run up the stairs. *Maybe I'll make it to the apartment,* I thought to myself.

I hit the stairs hard, even skipping steps at times. *Almost there, just around this rail and I will be home free.*

Just as I reached the top of the third floor landing I saw two other boys coming down towards me. One I had never seen before. He had a small baseball bat in his hand, like the souvenir bats you get at the ballpark. The other boy looked very familiar. With his face scarred and eyes still puffy, I recognized him immediately. It was the boy from my class at school, the one that was part of a rival gang; the one that my friends and I beat up. He still walked with a limp. In his hand was a silver and black 38 caliber pistol. I knew that type of gun well. It was my gun of choice.

What goes around comes around; and what you do to others, it will come back to you. I knew this to be true but I did not want to think about it at this time. All I wanted to think about was how to get out of this situation. But I couldn't. All I could think about was the fact that I was going to die and that it would be painful.

We never talked about this type of beating at the gang meetings that I attended in the 4848 building on the 13th floor. We never discussed the number of gang members that were killed each year. They told me how the gang would have my back if something happened to me. They told me how others would fear me and respect me.

But where were they now? No one was there with me besides these three angry young men that looked forward to bragging about how they shut Lil Fella up, permanently. There was no one there that had my back. The best they could do at this point was to avenge my death. For some reason, this was not very comforting at the time.

I don't recall which of those guys hit me first. I don't remember exactly how I ended up on the floor, curled in a fetal position. I do remember the stomps. It felt as if I was the turf under a marching band at a football field. It seemed to never stop. The bat cracking across my head, face and particularly my mouth produces a pain unlike I had ever felt before. As I felt my teeth being knocked out and my mouth filling with my own blood, I realized that this would be my last day on earth. They were not going to stop until I was dead.

Once the beating stopped, I could barely breathe. *I'm still alive.* I couldn't believe it. But then I realized it was not over. They were still there. As I pulled myself up to a kneeling position, I saw the gun. The young man I had beaten up held it to my face with a sense of satisfaction. As I heard the sound of him cocking the trigger, I braced myself for what I knew to be the inevitable. But the gun got stuck and did not go off.

"What the hell...", he exclaimed. He tried it again. The sound of the bullet rushing past my head was deafening. "Man, watch whatcha doing, you almost shot me", his brother screamed. "Come on, we gotta get outta here".

Although the sound of gunshots was common, it would definitely draw some type of unwanted attention. Not that anyone would rush to the stairwell to aid someone in need, but people would be looking. Eventually someone would wander in. This was to be avoided as much as possible.

They quickly tried to finish the job. By this time I was so weak and had lost so much blood, it would take but a few more punches to finish me off. As fists repeatedly landed in my face, I could feel my eyes swelling shut.

It was over. "He's done", I thought I heard one of them say. Or did I say it in my head? They left me there, assured within themselves that they had killed me. I laid there knowing that death was right around the corner.

The difference between greatness and mediocrity is often how an individual views a mistake.

Nelson Boswell

Chapter 2

I did not know at the time where my strength and determination to live came from. I remember pulling myself up on the stairs thinking if I could only make it to the door, I could get to my mom. By the time I reached the top of the stairway and somehow got through the door, I could feel my lungs struggling to operate. I could hardly breathe; it hurt too much. The burning in my lungs felt as if I had swallowed lit matches. My brain felt as if it was filled with fog. I couldn't think straight, couldn't keep my eyes opened. It felt like I was floating away.

Even in the face of all of this, I remembered the code of silence; don't tell and have nothing to say. How would I explain this? Perhaps I would not make it and then I would have nothing to explain. I would just be another statistic.

As my breath grew shorter and shorter, I could hear my mom frantically running and screaming, "My baby, somebody help me". The screams coming from my mother brought other people who gathered around me. Nosy neighbors, concerned family friends, and of course, other gang members crowded around to see my demise.

I did not feel or hear my mother near me anymore. When I finally heard her voice again she was saying that the paramedics were on their way. As she came closer to me she saw a mob of guys surrounding me. She didn't know what to say to them or even why they were there. I heard her say, "Who are you all and was my son with you? If he was, how did he get hurt with so many of you with him?"

It seemed as if everyone began talking at once. There were too many conversations for me to keep up with. My mother was screaming, "Who did this to you"? Other family members were crying or talking among themselves as to what they thought had happened. I did not answer, I couldn't. I felt myself slipping deeper and deeper out of consciousness.

I felt someone pick me up from the concrete. It seemed to take forever for the ambulance to come. With the broken elevator the paramedics would have to walk up 4 flights of stairs with a stretcher in hand. How long would that take, I wondered. That was not going to happen quickly I was sure of that. I am sure I passed out before help arrived. I have no memory of how long I was out. I didn't even know if I was dead or alive. I felt strange, not in as much pain but as if I was in a very deep sleep. Things felt far away from me. It was that feeling you have when you are really tired and can't keep your eyes open and your head up straight. That was the way I felt.

Once I arrived at the hospital, I heard sounds in the distance, but I had to strain to hear them. I did not know how bad I was hurt but I heard the doctors talking to each other very fast. I heard footsteps running away from the room. Whatever they were doing, it seemed like it was a lot of them working on me. Finally, I did not hear anybody. No voices, no sounds. I let go and drifted further to that place where I felt no pain only peace. As quickly as I drifted off to that peaceful place, I awoke to hear voices all around me. I later learned that I was in a coma.

It took a minute to know who was talking and what they were saying to me or to each other. The gang members wanted to know where the guns were. It seemed strange that they were only worried about where the guns were. I was not able to answer them right away, but I knew that the guns were safe, right under my bed, the same place they had been for months. I was so careful my mother didn't even have a clue that they were in her house.

It seemed like it was "business as usual" with my gang. They were making plans and these plans included me still being in the gang. I thought about my position in the gang. From what I heard it seemed like I still had my job. I was still the lookout man, and the one whose job it was to keep the guns stashed in a secret place.

They were so busy talking they didn't realize that I was awake. I surprised them by telling them where the guns were. My voice sounded so quiet I could barely hear it myself. I tried clearing my throat to make my voice louder but it didn't work. It was still low and real quiet.

I wanted to get a drink of water. Maybe that would make my voice stronger. *Never mind*, I thought to myself. I had already given them the answer they wanted, there was no need to say anything else right now. As I was drifting in and out of sleep, I noticed the gang members had left my room.

Finally, I was alone and conscious. I had time to think what was to happen next. I thought that I was going to die in that stairwell, but I didn't. This was not something I should be thinking about, after all I was only a kid. My time in the gang made me feel a lot older than I was, this life made me think far beyond my age. Having to spend so much time worrying about keeping safe, not being out there by myself, and being ready to fight when necessary, gave me a lot to think about. But at this moment I knew I would not have to deal with any of those things because I would be in this bed for a long time.

I found myself drifting off again. *Why was I sleeping so much?* I remembered that the Doctor gave me medicine for the pain. Soon that medicine would be wearing off. I hoped that they would give me more. I sure didn't want to deal with that pain again.

I guess those guys really beat me down. I felt stiff like I ran up and down the stairs. It felt as if every muscle in my body was affected. I didn't even want to look under the bandages. That would only make me mad, mad enough to make plans to pay them back. I couldn't heal fast enough. I had to get out of here. They would pay for what they did to me.

I started thinking what would have happened if I had seen those guys before I went into the stairway. If only I had not been by myself, if only, if only, if only. None of that mattered now. I had plans. *I'm gonna kill them all.*

Now I have to deal with my mother. I was sure she would return to the hospital soon with a million questions. I was not ready to tell her what she wanted to know but I had to tell her something. This is one of the first times probably in my whole life that I didn't want to talk. I had time to come up with a story that she would buy, and everything would be okay.

Early the next morning I got a visit from the Chicago Police Department. Of course they wanted to know who did this to me and why they did it. They asked the usual questions, as if they really cared. It did not matter how they questioned me or tried to scare me, I did not give them anything. Nothing. As they left they placed a card on the table with the station phone number on it. They told me that if I remembered anything, I should call them. After they left, I tore the card up. I didn't want anyone thinking that I was talking to the police.

As the officers were leaving my food tray was being brought into the room. I thought to myself, *Man, I am hungry.* I sat up in the bed so that I could eat my food. It didn't look very appetizing, but I was very hungry. I opened the top that was on the plate and piled some food on the fork. As the fork touched my lips I noticed that my lips felt at least 2 sizes bigger than usual. I also realized how difficult it is to eat without your front teeth. Although my gums were still swollen, that did not stop me from eating. I could not remember the last time I had eaten anything.

After breakfast, the nurse came into the room to check on me. She told me that the doctor would be in soon to see me. He had to check out my bruises and make sure that I did not get worse overnight. Since nobody had told me anything about my injuries, I wanted to hear what the doctor had to say.

As I was waiting for the doctor to come, I had another visitor. It was the Governor. The "Governor" as we called him, was one of the leaders of the gang. He told me how proud he was of me. He also wanted to know who did this to me. I knew what this meant. Whoever did this to me would be killed.

I knew they would want to avenge me. It felt good to know that someone thought I was important enough to kill for. As much as I wanted to enjoy this feeling, it seemed as if my conscience screamed, "Stop it. This is not right". Oh how I had wanted them to die. I felt enough rage to want to kill them myself. But at the same time there seemed to be a war raging inside of me. I had no idea at the time where this opposing thought, this sense of civility was coming from. I didn't understand what was happening in my mind. *Perhaps it's the drugs,* I thought. Just as I was trying to find something to say to him, my mom came in the door.

She looked at the Governor. She did not say anything to him. She spoke directly to me, "How do you know this man? I heard he just got out of prison." The Governor boldly told my mom, "Oh, he is one of my foot soldiers." When he said that, I peeked at my mom out of the corner of my eye.

"Is that true?" she said as she put her hands on her hips. Mary Perkins was not a woman to be played with. Being the third oldest of seven girls, my mom was no push over and she did not scare easily. Having 11 children of her own, 6 boys and 5 girls made her tough in her own right. Although she was small in stature, she could be a force to reckon with.

I didn't answer her. I knew one day I would have to answer that question, I just wasn't ready to right now.

Out of the blue, the Governor asked me, right in front of my mother. "Where are the guns, I need them?" I knew I had to answer him; after all he was the Governor, one of the most powerful positions in the gang. I felt as if a flood gate had opened. I had never felt so overwhelmed before. *What am I doing?* It was at that moment that I realized that this whole business of being in a gang was much more than I had bargained for. This man was powerful enough to hurt me and my entire family.

I had to answer right then. I told them that they were in a locked box under my bed at home. I had already told the gang members the same thing. They didn't tell me they needed them right away like the Governor did. I knew I had to turn them over to him right away. Well, not I, but my mother would have to give them to him.

My mom just stood there, with a look of surprise and amazement on her face. I knew she was scared, but that was not going to stop her from talking.   At first her voice sounded real shaky. "You have guns stored, in my house?" She said quietly, almost as if she were talking to herself. "In my house... under my roof...". All of a sudden her voice began to get loud and strong.   She looked at the Governor and said, "I will give you anything you want if you let my son go."   I knew what she meant; she was asking him to let me out of the gang.

The Governor didn't say anything at first.   I think that he was amazed that this little woman would be bold enough to even make such a proposition.   Of course she was going to give him the guns.   She would not tell the police or anyone else if she knew what was best for her and her family.   He looked at my mother with a slight grin on his face.   "I'll be by there in a bit", he told her.   He looked back at me and told me to take care of myself.   He left the room.

My mother looked at me with such hurt in her eyes.   I have never seen her look that way before.   "Lawrence Joseph Perkins, Jr", she said.   "Have you lost your mind?"   Her voice began to rise again but not too loud as to draw attention.   You could sense the frustration she felt.   She seemed to get desperate and started to pray.   Yes, pray, out loud right there in the room.   It was the first time I had ever heard my mother pray.   She begged and pleaded with God to help her get me out of this mess I had made for myself and to get me out of the gang.   I was so surprised when I heard her pray.   I will always remember that moment.   I knew that she was sincere.

Although I had never heard her pray before, she looked like she had done this type of prayer before. I heard her use words like "Father please, forgive him", "send your angels to watch over him", and "like your Word said that You would". She said more than one time the words "In the name of Jesus". That really made me pay attention. I was only accustomed to religious people using the name of God and Jesus. Although I was not involved in any type of church at the time, I had heard that there were people who talked to God and things happened for them. I was curious to see if God would answer my mother's prayer.

She finally finished praying and turned to me with tears in her eyes. "You need to change your life now or these guys or some other ones will kill you. This time is a wakeup call." She reached out, touched my hand and looked me straight in my eyes. Her eyes were full of sorrow and compassion. "Warnings come before destruction". As she said these words I could feel chills down my back.

I could not take it anymore. I told my mother that I wanted out of the gang. I explained to her that I didn't have a reason to get out. "I wanted attention from you and daddy but neither of you had time for me. I got in the gang knowing that I had to "die out", it didn't matter, what did I have to lose?" Tears began to stream down my face.

The whole room got completely silent, both of us just sat there not talking or looking at each other, for what seemed like hours, but was only a few minutes. My mother got up and left the room.

A wave of anxiety suddenly overtook me. My thoughts were racing. I could feel sweat on my forehead. I had to calm down. I took some deep breaths in order to slow my heart beat down. My heart was beating so fast, I thought I would die right that minute. I started to breathe in and let it out slowly. I did this a few times and finally felt a little better. I thought about that prayer again. I still did not know if it would do any good. I know what she was asking for had never happened before. I expected to "die out". I wasn't ready to die, but I didn't know any other way to get out.

Later that evening as I was thinking about my "die out" option, my mother walked back into my hospital room. She stood by my bed and said, "That Governor said you are out of the gang. I turned those lock boxes over to him a little while ago."

I felt a sense of relief like I had never felt before. I would not have to "die out". I could actually walk by them on the street and not be marked as a traitor.

"Thank you momma", I said. "I'm sorry", I added.

"Don't worry about it", she said. "But don't ever do anything that stupid again. Next time you might not be so lucky".

I knew she was right. As I laid there I thought about the prayer. *I guess that prayer stuff does work sometimes.* I thought to myself. *I have my life back.* Just then I could hear another voice in my mind. *Yeah, what life? No gang means no friends. You can't hang with them anymore. They don't have your back no more. What will you belong to now?*

I left the hospital a few days later, after being there for about 3 weeks.

There is greatness in the fear of God, contentment in faith of God, and honour in humility.

Abu Bakr

Chapter 3

After I left the hospital from my near death beat down, my mother forced me to live with my aunt for a few months. She lived in the West Pullman neighborhood on the south side of Chicago. This place seemed like a whole new world. Instead of large, towering, high rise projects with urine filled halls and broken elevators, there were single family homes on pristine lots and manicured lawns. I couldn't believe that only one family lived in these homes. There was enough room for at least 3 or 4 families based on where I was from.

A person can move from one physical environment to another. However, if there is no change in that person's heart, their character or their outlook on life, they are destined to experience the same problems they had before they moved locations. I was physically away from the gangs and the projects but the gangs and projects were still a part of me. All I did was change location. As a result, I found myself in as much trouble at my aunt's home as I did when I was in the projects.

After the summer, I returned to the Robert Taylor Homes. This was home to me. This was where I found my version of peace. As school was beginning again, some of the summer violence was tapering off. Things had calmed down for me. The guys that almost killed me had moved out of the projects by then. Things were "normal", whatever that was.

According the dictionary, a metamorphosis is a "profound change in form from one stage to the next in the life history of an organism, as from the caterpillar to the pupa and from the pupa to the adult butterfly." Without this "profound change", a caterpillar would remain just that, a caterpillar; crawling around on the ground and leaves, never fulfilling its destiny to be a butterfly.

My metamorphosis began after I moved back from my aunt's. Having survived the gangs and the beatings, I was still just a caterpillar. I had no direction for my life and did not even realize it. I was just going along for the ride.

One of my best friends, Dips, asked me one day if I wanted to go to church with him. Dips was previously a member of a rival gang but had gotten out. I had never been in a church before except for funerals. *Why not*, I thought to myself. *What do I have to lose?*

Dips's pastor came to pick us up in his blue, 4 door, Chevy Caprice. The car was filled with other young people from the projects. Since I was extremely thin, it wasn't hard for me to sit on someone's lap. I don't know if there were any seat belt laws back then. If you were lucky enough to have a car, you could ride as many people as could fit.

Ridin' in style. Guess not just gang bangers have cars. Preachers do too, I thought to myself. *One day I'm gonna have a ride like this.*

We pulled up to the church. It was located in the Greater Grand Crossing area in Chicago. This was another area of the city that I had never been to before. Although this was much closer to where I lived, it still looked like a different city. There were stores with apartments on top.

These storefronts housed everything from churches to liquor stores.

The church was small but it was filled with people, many of whom were young people from the projects. "Hey, whatsup", I nodded to a few guys that I knew. As I looked around, I realized that I had seen many of these kids before. I also realized that most of them knew me, or at least had heard about me. I had a reputation.

The music was fantastic. I had never seen live music before. It was great, but it was loud. I mean really, really loud. There were huge speakers hanging from the walls on each side of the room. This made the organ and drums seem even louder. It didn't bother me since I was accustomed to loud music. It was actually quite fascinating.

The choir began to sing. They sang with a joy and emotion that I had never seen before. They were waving their hands and crying but it did not feel as if they were sad. They were, as I found out later, "praising God".

As the music got faster, the subtle hand waves and crying grew more and more intense. People were standing and clapping their hands to the music. It felt joyous. I felt joyous, good on the inside but I knew that I could not show it. I was taught by the gang members to be tough, not show a lot of emotions. But I felt good. That was something I had not felt in a long time.

All of a sudden, there were screams. "Thank you Jesus"! "Hallelujah"! Someone jumped up and started to dance.

"What is that?", I laughed hunching Dips. "Hush", he hunched me back. "Stop laughing".

I tried to stop but I couldn't. It was too funny. In all of my 14 years on this earth, I had never seen anything like this.

"What kinda dance is that"? I said, trying to contain my laughter.

"Stop it, I told you", Dips said. But I could tell that he was laughing a little also.

"I bet ya a dolla that lady's hat is gonna fall off", I shrugged Dips. "Bet", said Dips.

That hat didn't move. It was like it was stuck with Super Glue. That lady jumped, ran up and down the aisles and then did some type of shuffle thing with her feet. The hat still did not move.

Then the young people started doing the same type of dance. I just sat back and quietly laughed to myself. It was entertaining but it also made me feel strange. Not a bad strange, but strange all the same. Through all of the laughing and joking, I could sense that those people, even the kids, had something that I didn't have. I didn't know what it was at the time but it was something.

After the dance party, the Pastor got up to welcome everyone to the church. This was the first time I got a real good look at him. Pastor Agee was a short, dark complexioned gentleman with a humble smile and character. Most women would probably consider him attractive.

The Pastor asked everyone to open their Bibles. *Bible?* I did not have a Bible but the person next to me allowed me to share theirs. *Please don't call on me to read!* Panic set in for a moment. My reading skills were really bad at the time. Luckily, he read the passage himself.

His message was from the Book of Acts. Pastor Agee talked about the conversion of Saul to Paul. He told us how God knocked Saul off his horse because he tried to destroy the church. Saul would go around imprisoning, beating and even killing people because they were Christians and he was not.

The thing that intrigued me about Saul was that he was not doing these activities illegally. He had the backing of the government at that time. He was like a gang banging policeman. That was cool in my mind.

The Pastor went on to explain the encounter Saul had with Jesus. He read how Saul was blinded and how his life was changed for good.

I thought to myself, *if God could change Saul's life, He could do the same thing for me.* By the end of the service I began to feel a change on the inside of me. I did not know then exactly what it was. I realize now that a seed had been planted in my heart.

Pastor Agee concluded his sermon by "opening the doors of the church" and asking if anyone wanted to join the church and give their life to God. Being in church for the first time, I was waiting for someone to open up the doors in the back of the church. Dips leaned over and whispered, "Here's your chance to make a change in your life".

Why not? I got out of my chair and started walking down the aisle toward Pastor Agee. It took forever; it seemed, to walk down that aisle. People were clapping and screaming "Amen". That made me a little nervous but I kept walking. I didn't look back. At that moment, it didn't matter what was going on around me. I had this incredible urge to keep moving forward. I really did not understand at the time what I was doing. I had no idea what "know God for yourself" really meant. I just knew that I needed to do something different and I needed to belong to something.

I finally got to the front of the church with Pastor Agee. He asked me, in front of the whole congregation, "Why do you want to be saved"?

"I'm tired of living a bad life and if God could change Saul to Paul, he could change me too".

Everyone started clapping even louder.

"What is your name" the Pastor asked.

"Lil Fella", I replied.

"Your real name", he said.

"Lawrence", I answered. "Lawrence Perkins".

The pastor said, "When I anoint you, God will change you from the inside out and from this point forward you will not be called Lil Fella. You will be called Lawrence Perkins. The old you has gone away and you will be born again".

I did not know what most of that meant at the time. The pastor laid his hands on me and anointed me with oil. Oil and tears began to run down my face. Something was happening to me. I did not know what but something felt different on the inside.

Pastor Agee touched my shoulder and looked me straight in my eyes. I could feel a sense of compassion and love but also boldness. No one had ever looked at me so intently. "God has a plan for your life. God is calling you to be a leader and not a follower. If you go back to your old ways of life and do not change, the devil is going to kill you."

That scared the hell out of me. It was something about what he said that nearly scared me to death. I was not a person that scared easily. I joined a gang knowing that I could get killed being a part of it or get killed trying to leave it. But something about what Pastor Agee said really shook me up. It reminded me of what my mother said about "warning coming before destruction".

As Pastor Agee touched me again, I experienced what I now know to be the baptism of the Holy Ghost. I joined the church and attended church every Sunday. I gave the pastor my hand and God my heart.

True greatness consists in being great in little things.

Charles Simmons

Chapter 4

Metamorphosis is a process. It does not occur overnight. Most lasting change does not. It takes time to break old habits and old mindsets. The same was with me. Although the Pastor told me that "God would change me from the inside out", that change did not happen right away.

Some things did change right away. I stopped slouching my pants below my butt. I enrolled in high school and decided to take school "a little more seriously". To me "a little more seriously" meant at least trying to make it to class.

Since I was not gifted academically, DuSable High School was the only choice for me. It was located across the street from the housing complex I lived in. DuSable was the neighborhood school where all of my friends and enemies went as well.   During this time, DuSable had a dropout rate of 58%.

DuSable High School was built in 1934 as an expansion of another high school in the area. It is named after Chicago's first permanent non-native settler, Jean Baptiste Point du Sable. In the 1930's and 1940's, DuSable High School was known for its music program, under the direction of Captain Walter Dyett. That program turned out a number of notable jazz musicians and singers such as Gene Ammons, Ronnie Boykins, Nat "King" Cole, Dorothy Donegan, Ella Jenkins, and Dinah Washington. DuSable also boasts of other famous alumni including Harold Washington, Chicago's first black mayor, NBA player Maurice Cheeks, and television personalities like Don Cornelius and Redd Fox.

As a freshman, I was still trying to find myself. I was no longer the gang banger, the look-out man for my gang. However, I was no little angel either. My new found religion offered some direction but it was not enough. Since my parents did not attend church, these new values that I was acquiring were not being instilled at home. I found myself still trying to escape the drugs, gangs and violence.

My quest to discover who I was got a kick start one fall morning in 1983. I walked into the third floor boy's bathroom and found a group of my old friends hanging out, passing around a 40 ounce bottle of malt liquor. I could still smell the weed that I must have missed a few minutes earlier. *Man, I should have gotten in here earlier.*

"Com'on boy, you better git some of this", one of my friends said, handing the bottle to me.

"Man, it's too early for this. First period hasn't even started yet", I said jokingly, steady reaching for the bottle.

As soon as I got the bottle in my hands, a teacher screamed, "Dr. Hamberlin, come in through that door and I'll get this one."

"Not Doc", one of the guys said. "Let's get outta here".

There were about 10 of us. We ran toward the voice we heard. No one wanted to experience "Doc's wrath". We would rather take our chances with this other guy.

I was toward the back of the crowd. We all tried to run past the teacher. Most of us got out except for Bardell, David and myself.

"Young man," the teacher screamed, "why aren't you guys in class?"

I did not know the teacher, Mr. Richardson, but I had seen him around before. The word around school was that he was cool, someone you could talk to if you got into trouble. But he wasn't that cool. There was no way I could talk my way out of this. I had the bottle in my hand and you could still smell the joint that was lit earlier that I missed.

"You're going to be suspended today", Mr. Richardson screamed, "We're going to the principal's office right now."

Bardell and David just stood there like deer caught in the headlights. I was going to have to come up with something. I could not get kicked out of school.

"Mr. Richardson, if you take me to the principal they are going to put me out of this school! Don't you want to see a black boy get his education?" I began to plead my case. "Please! Mr. Richardson give us a break."

He did not look like he was buying it. However, instead of taking me and my friends to the principal's office, which would have required loads of paperwork, Mr. Richardson had me to help organize books in his office. He also made us agree to participate in his debate team class after school, with the promise that if we missed one day, he would take us to the principal's office.

I was thankful that he did not take me to the principal's office. I would have been suspended immediately. My mother would have killed me.

Soon, Bardell and I began hanging around Mr. Richardson's office on a regular basis. This gave me a little since of responsibility. I felt important. I had not felt like that since my days in the gang.

Bardell, or BW as we called him, was a soft spoken boy who had narrow eyes and a golden complexion. This led to plenty of teasing by other students that he was part Chinese. BW had also played with the idea of joining a gang.

BW and I complemented each other perfectly. I was excitable and garrulous. I talked excessively, often rambling about trivial issues. BW, on the other hand was calm and reticent. He was much more reserved and didn't talk about his feelings often.

Under the guidance of Mr. Richardson, we really began to take school more seriously. Not only did we go to class, we tried to do better in our classes. This was a challenge since neither of us was academically gifted. We did join the debate team and, at Mr. Richardson urging, wrote for the school's literary magazine.

As part of the debate team, we would travel to high schools in some of the wealthiest suburbs of Chicago, including Downers Grove, Niles, New Trier, and Stevenson High School. Those trips inspired me. I began to want more out of life than I had previously experienced.

On one debate trip to a tournament in one of Chicago's wealthiest suburb's, after a very tough round, we discovered that I had won the round over one of the district's top debaters. That excited me more than anyone could imagine. "I am as good as those white boys", I shouted! "I can be anything I want to be!"

The metamorphosis was accelerating. We really changed how we presented ourselves at school. We started carrying briefcases and I even began wearing ties. We started spending afternoons at the local library. Other students started referring to me as Preach since they said I would start sermonizing in the hallways.

We started carrying a Bible nearly every day to school. BW would go to church initially just for the free sandwiches. However, the church became a solid pillar of support for us. In our community, the foundation had crumbled.

Mr. Richardson often told us that we were ready to consider college but we didn't believe him. BW and I would talk about it as if it were a fantasy.

"Wouldn't it be cool to go to Alcorn State University like Dr. Hamberlin"? BW asked one day.

"That would be awesome", I said.

"Can you imagine living on a college campus?" he asked.

"Not really. I don't know if we could do it. We better be thinking about getting a job right here. We can't afford college no way. Besides, the way I write and talk...I'm better off staying right here", I told him.

"I hear ya", BW said.

College. No one in my family had ever been to college. I had not really thought seriously about college until Mr. Richardson started talking to us about it. Sure, I had survived the gangs and made it through elementary and high school, but college! That was beyond my imagination.

I think the biggest encouragement I had for going to college came from the belief that Mr. Richardson had in me. Mr. Richardson had become like a father to me. He knew me well. He knew my strengths and my weaknesses. I trusted his opinion. He told me that he thought I could do this. Not only could I do it but I owed it to myself to do it. I had survived some things that others hadn't. I was here for a reason.

I looked up to Mr. Richardson. When he told me, "Go for it boy, make your dreams come true", I felt that I could really do it. Mr. Richardson was one of the first people to help me see that there were seeds of greatness in me. I could achieve my dreams. He believed in me. It was time for me to believe in myself.

At the end of my junior year, I considered the idea of running for senior class president with BW as my vice president. Just as everyone knew me when I was gang banging in the neighborhood, everyone knew me at DuSable. I was extremely popular. Mr. Richardson suggested putting together a slate for the five class offices, all males. DuSable had not seen anything like that for years.

Girls were traditionally the valedictorians and ran the student government. Mr. Richardson thought this would be a good chance to show that boys could do it as well. So we ran and won the election with 98% of the votes.

During my senior year of high school I became saturated with courses of interest such as Horticulture, Journalism, Debating, Reserve Officer Training Corps (ROTC) and music. Although I loved to talk, I had difficultly using "proper" English. I was put in a program to help address some of these deficits. This contributed to my interest in public speaking.

As senior class president, I had the opportunity to encourage my fellow students to excel. It was during this time that I received my first recognition as a role model in the community.   I received a plaque for Outstanding Achievement from Fay Terrell Perkins, who served as the Chicago Board of Education's Director of Vocation Education, and Norman Colmesa from radio station WVON.

I was featured a number of times in local newspapers such as the Chicago Defender and the Chicago Tribune. I also had the opportunity to participate in a number of community celebrations, such as DuSable Celebrates King's Birthday and African American History month with the late

Mayor Harold Washington. Mayor Washington was the first African American mayor of Chicago, as well as a graduate of DuSable High School.

Shortly before my senior graduation, I received a letter from the city of Chicago. In it was a letter from Mayor Harold Washington. It read:

Dear Lawrence,

The People of Chicago celebrate your achievement – YOUR RECENT GRADUATION! This is a milestone in your life, and you've worked hard for your diploma. Your achievement is a credit to you personally, your family and friends, and to all of the People of Chicago. Congratulations, I am proud of your accomplishment.

It was signed by Mayor Washington.

I felt like I was on top of the world.

Although my focus on school had improved dramatically, I was still distracted by many things including the availability of drugs, peer pressure and the opposite sex. Although I considered myself a decent Christian young man, the idea of abstinence was just that, an idea. Since I believed that everyone was "doing it", having pre-marital sex did not present a moral dilemma for me. Besides, I figured that there were many people out there doing far worse than I was. They seemed to get along just fine.

Along with making a few bad "moral" choices, I also found myself making some common sense errors. I quickly realized that there were consequences for every choice that I made. Sometimes, though, it seemed as if I got away when I made a poor choice. However, there were other times that I didn't.

When the young lady that I was "fooling around" with told me that she was pregnant, I couldn't believe it. *I'm only 17*, I thought to myself. *How could this happen? This was the only time I didn't use protection.*

I had a serious decision to make. I had three months left of my senior year of high school. Would I go to college or stay home and get a job so that I could help support my child? I chose to go to college. I realized that I did not have a clue what it required to raise a child. I wondered, how would I support this child since I was just a child myself and living with my parents?

Because of my family upbringing, I knew that I would have to take responsibility. I also knew that quitting school was not an option. I firmly believed that I needed to do something to make sure that I set up a secure foundation to support this child. It was not an easy decision and many did not agree with it at the time.

Man's greatness lies in his power of thought.

Blaise Pascal

Chapter 5

Mr. Richardson raised the money just like he had promised to get BW and me down to Alcorn State University. Alcorn was about 1,000 miles away from Chicago in Lorman, Mississippi. We never talked about where Mr. Richardson got the money. He was a man of his word. He came through for us.

I was so excited the night before leaving I stayed up all night. I never thought that I would be leaving the Robert Taylor Homes heading for college, or anyplace else for that matter. I was thinking about a whole new city, new people, new dreams, a life of independence from my parents and other family members. Although this new life would be full of responsibilities, adult decisions and choices, I would still find time to see the sights and enjoy college life.

Just thinking about things made me very anxious to get on the road. My leaving was a bittersweet moment. I was sad to go, but glad to leave. Robert Taylor projects had nothing for me anymore. I escaped with my life and my dreams and the possibility of a good future.

I was certainly sad to leave my family, but, I had to follow my dreams. Actually I wasn't leaving my entire family, my best friend BW was going with me. We planned to look out for each other, study together, and do whatever it took to make our parents and people like Mr. Richardson and Dr. Hamberlin proud of us. We had to enroll at Alcorn State during the summer session, since we had several areas that we needed to catch up on. Getting there before the more crowded session would be an advantage for us. We needed to get a certificate in order to complete our enrollment.

I thought about how we were going to accomplish all of these things to get in. The school officials were aware of our situation and were waiting to meet with us upon our arrival. This was going to be a long, exciting trip. I looked out of the apartment window constantly while waiting for Mr. Richardson to pick me up and then go a few blocks up to 55th and Prairie to pick up BW.

Getting away from my neighborhood during the summer months was a very good idea. The possibilities of getting into trouble, going to jail or maybe even getting killed was much greater in the summer. I looked at the clock one last time before going to the window to look out for Mr. Richardson.

Finally, he's here. I looked at him as he got out of the car. He had actually rented a car just for this trip. As he drove up to the building gang members and other people ran up to his car to meet him. Everybody was out there this morning. It was not common for a teacher to come into the projects. Many of those standing around were ones he tried to save, too. Unfortunately, some of them were lost to the streets. Mr. Richardson made his way to the elevator and up to apartment #408. I met him at the door with a big smile on my face. This man was making a great investment into my future.

"Take care of my baby. Please don't let anything happen to him," my mother said as she spoke to Mr. Richardson. With concern and sadness in her eyes, she reached into her purse and took out a book of foodstamps worth $60.00. She wanted to make sure that we were not going to be without food. I picked up all of my things and headed for the door. After saying my goodbyes to my family, we headed for the elevator. This would be my last time for a while having to wonder if the elevator would be working. I looked back a couple of times at my past, while walking towards my future. Gone were the days of fighting, days of fear and getting in trouble. I really was not very sad to see an end to those things.

Next, we went to pick up BW. He only lived a short distance from me on 55th and Prairie. His family was fortunate to move out of Robert Taylor a few months earlier. Mr. Richardson pulled up in front of BW's house. We both got out of the car to go in. BW's mother opened the door. Her eyes were red and puffy from crying. She was really saddened about his leaving, but she understood that his leaving was necessary. BW's mother gave him $45.00 worth of foodstamps for the trip. This gave us a total of $105.00, more than enough to fill our stomachs for a few days. BW threw his clothes into the car and jumped in. He looked back as we left the block and headed for the expressway. I am sure that he, too, had his own silent thoughts of what was ahead of him.

The excitement of our first trip outside of Chicago gave us energy to talk all day about what college would be like. We knew that we had a long ride ahead of us and plenty of time to rest, if we wanted too. We excitedly looked out of the car windows at real animals. We had only seen animals at the zoo. That, in itself, was an experience for us. Well, just about everything was at this point. We had only seen things surrounding our neighborhood. What we knew was so limited. This trip would change the rest of our lives.

The trip was even longer than we expected because we got lost. That just gave us even more to talk about. We didn't have cell phones or GPS systems at that time so we had to figure out where we were. We stopped for directions and got back on the right road. It was my plan to stay awake all the way there, but I found myself waking up just before we arrived in front of the campus. *We are actually here, Alcorn State University,* I thought as we all got out of the car and looked around smiling.

The campus was beautiful. It looked like something on a postcard. We were surprised to see that the campus and everything around it was so clean. We were not sure where the building we needed to go to was located. Mr. Richardson stopped some students that were walking by and asked where the registration office was located. The students were so friendly and helpful. This made me proud that I would soon be enrolled here. We were surprised to see some of the students carrying brief cases and that they were so polite to each other. This was something that neither of us was used to seeing. We followed the directions that we were given and finally made it to the registration office. The people in this office were polite as well.

One of the directors in the Registrar's office sat down with us. After he looked at the folder that contained our information, he looked up and stated, "Bardell can start classes this summer. He had met the requirements for admissions." The gentleman gave BW the form he needed to complete enrollment. He would be able to get his room key and his student ID card. That ID also served as his meal card. He would be able to have meals with the other students in the cafeteria starting today.

The director looked over at me. He said, "I regret that you are unable to enroll today." He explained that my ACT scores were too low. He didn't tell me right away what I needed to do. He turned to Mr. Richardson and said, "You will have to take Lawrence back to Chicago with you. He can come back in thirty days; retake the ACT test to get a higher score. If his score is at the level our university requires we will enroll him then."

As we walked out of the office a great sense of sorrow overwhelmed me. I thought to myself, *I don't want to go back to Chicago. I don't want to go back even for a little while and have to take that long drive back here in a month.* Besides, I did not want to leave BW there all by himself. BW did not want to stay there by himself either. I turned to Mr. Richardson and said "I can't go back to Chicago because I will get into trouble." I knew exactly what going back would do to me. I had already been approached to sell drugs and get with the gang members before I left there. Finding trouble was always easy. Most of the people I knew all did the same kinds of things to keep busy.

I said, "Please, please Mr. Richardson. Just let me stay here with BW. I need to stay here. If I stay here, I can study on campus. I will have plenty of time and will not be distracted by people who don't want to see me get in school. I have to stay here. I can't go back to Chicago." I knew how important staying there on campus would be for me. Staying on campus would be part of my inspiration to get the scores that I needed to be able to enroll in the school.

I was finally able to convince Mr. Richardson to leave me there. He probably saw the sincerity and determination in my face. We spent a few more minutes talking to each other. As Mr. Richardson got into his car, he gave both of us a hug. He said if either of us needed anything, we could feel free to give him a call. His final words were that he would be praying for us.

That night we both held hands and prayed. We prayed that God would help us and that His will would be done. When we finished praying, we realized that I had no real place to stay and no plans as to how I would be able to do the things I needed to do to get ready for the test. This was turning into a big challenge. It was one that I was not willing to give up on.

I told BW, "We can't look backwards, that is the past. We are only going to deal with those things in the present and look to our future. We will make it." BW replied," I am my brother's keeper. You can sleep on the floor in my room."

I was determined to do whatever was necessary to overcome this challenge. The thoughts began invading my mind. *I can clean the dormitory halls to earn money so that I can eat. I may even be able to get a job in the cafeteria so I can eat free.* I have always known how to be resourceful. I would manage my time and get everything that I needed. I would study hard and prepare myself to retake the tests, pass them and complete my enrollment. This was no time to become passive, my aggressive nature had kicked in and I started to figure out what I would need to do to make my plan work out.

I knew that I had to get in the library to study. With all of the books there, it would be easier to have what I need right at my fingertips. It never dawned on me that I was on campus, living illegally. We talked for a while longer and finally fell off to sleep. I slept long and hard. I don't recall if I had dreamt that night.

When I woke up the next morning, I took off running. I had to speak to the right people in order to get my plan into action. First I talked to the person in charge of the dormitory. I told him about my plans to stay there and retake my ACTs so I could complete my enrollment for the fall semester. I think he saw my drive and determination, so he let me clean the dorm areas two days per week in exchange for letting me stay in BW's room.

Next, I talked to the cafeteria manager hoping to make a deal there also. I hoped that he would allow me to clean the cafeteria in exchange for 2 free meals a day. The manager agreed. I cleaned at night after the cafeteria closed. The manager also allowed me to take leftover food to the dorms so that I would have food to eat later each night.

My next task would be to meet with the person in charge of the library. I explained to her my problem and that I really needed to come to the library to study. I needed her help to gain access to the facility, since to get into the library I needed a school ID which I did not have yet. She agreed. I was given authorization to use the library facilities, but could not take any of the books off the premises.

When I wasn't cleaning up, I was studying, day in and day out. Those thirty days passed so quickly. I used this time to really focus as I was preparing to take the test. I was nervous but I knew that this was my chance to pass, and I was ready.

I did all of the things I had heard for taking a test. First, take a deep breath, get focused, block out everything around you that would be a distraction. If I didn't know the answer right then, I should skip it and come back to it later. I knew not to waste time because time was precious. This test was being timed. The more questions I answered the better my chances of passing. The clock was ticking. When I heard the person giving the test say "stop and put your pencils down", I prayed that I had successfully completed my task.

I felt pretty good as I left the test area. It would take a while before I knew my results. I was hopeful though.

The day finally arrived. I was told that my scores were sufficient for admission. I was finally able to officially enroll as a student at Alcorn State University.

Great men are not always wise...

The Holy Bible – Job 32:9

Chapter 6

Once I was enrolled as an official student at Alcorn State, the real work began. I was excited when I received my scores from the ACT test. These scores made me know that I was ready for the challenge of pursuing a B.A. Degree. I guess I had to go through having low test scores to help me to work hard and take my studies seriously. I would have to be focused and consistent.

I knew that I needed to manage my time by setting up a schedule that would allow me to do all of the things I needed to do, especially study. Although I was able to register for classes, many of those classes were remedial level courses. These classes were designed to start at a lower level setting the groundwork needed to cover things that I missed in high school. Two of my major courses were reading and writing. I understood the importance of getting on the right level in both of these classes. I would be unable to complete the required classes if I did not excel in the remedial classes.

Just to be at Alcorn State University was a dream come true. I knew that in order to reach my dream of being the first college graduate in my family I had to do some things, ask for some things and give up some things to walk across that stage in the next few years.

I was experiencing two firsts in my family even though I was the youngest child of 11. I was the first to attend college and live away from home. What are the odds of this happening to a young man from the South Side of Chicago in the Robert Taylor Projects? I could have made some choices that would have precluded me from sitting in that dorm room. Reflecting on this truth made me feel a sense of gratitude to Mr. Richardson. He was very instrumental in making it possible for me to have that chance.

It was my desire to take that opportunity and make the best of it. I studied hard, went to the library, and did not skip classes. I became more serious and diligent than I had ever been in my life. This was not the time to slack off. I started off behind so I had to catch up.

Even though I had challenges with getting on course and keeping my grades up, I wanted to get involved in activities going on around me. Life on a college campus was exciting. There was always something going on even during the weekdays. I wanted to go to some of the parties and other events. I decided that I would go out and see what students did to have some fun. There were lots of campus groups recruiting new members, especially fraternities and sororities.

The frat members would be outside especially during the warm days "steppin". They did this so that people would want to pledge their group. They were smooth. There were many groups out there. I had actually considered pledging a fraternity but I couldn't because of my GPA.

It was probably best that I wasn't able to pledge the fraternity. The pledging process reminded me somewhat of the gang initiation process. Now don't get me wrong. Most Greek organizations are awesome. They do tremendous work for the community and provide a sense of leadership and guidance to many young people during a very critical time in their lives. However, as an onlooker from the outside, the hazing process did remind me a little of gang initiation. Similar to a gang, the fraternity had things you had to do to get in to show your allegiance to the club. They expected you to be on call when they wanted you; they made you do foolish things just to test you. All of this was just to be considered for membership. There were also colors and handshakes that were particular to each fraternity. Although I don't believe that you had to take 50 punches to the chest in order to become part of a fraternity, there were some physical things that occurred, at least on the undergraduate level. Both of these groups had another thing in common, you were a member for the rest of your life. Did I really want to give up my freedom, personality, and identity again? No thanks!

It became a moot point. Even if I wanted to join, I couldn't. Besides, pledging would take me away from the study routine I had so carefully developed. I am sure to other students in the dorm and on campus I appeared to be bookworm. People in the dorm would comment that the only thing they saw me do is study. They wanted to know when I had fun. I told them that I got out every now and then, but I had a goal to complete and fun had to be in second place. Good grades came easy for some people; I had to work extremely hard for them.

I never expected college to be easy. Getting good grades were always hard for me. I was the type of student who had personality. Having personality always seemed to get me places. I had what people called "the gift of gab". I could talk the average person into seeing and doing things my way most of the time. I had charisma. I was well liked and popular. These characteristics covered up the fact that I was not a very good student. My teachers liked me, so did most of the students in my classes. I believe that they were not aware of my failure to achieve scores at my grade level.

I knew the truth all too well, and had to study harder and longer than the average student. I needed to succeed, I needed to pass, but most importantly, I needed to graduate college. I planned to dedicate this degree to all the kids who wanted to attend college but couldn't, wouldn't or had been told they shouldn't. I worked harder for the family of kids that were killed before reaching age 15 and would never attend college.

After years of study and sacrifice, graduation day finally arrived. So many people were on my mind as I walked across the stage to receive my degree. I smiled thinking about my best friend Dips, my family members and anyone else who helped me get there. I was particularly happy to have my son there. I have always given his mother the utmost respect and recognition for raising our son without my presence those five years while I was attending college.

However, my heart was not worry free. It has been said that if you do not learn the lesson that a situation in life has to teach you, you will experience similar situations until you learn the lesson. Here I was, in my senior year of school, facing the same situation again. I was about to become a father, again. Although the situation was very different, it was very much the same. I was leaving. I was not staying in Mississippi. My career plans were in Chicago. I knew what my decision would be. It would appear arrogant and immature. Perhaps it was.

Do not despise the bottom rungs in the ascent to greatness.

Publilius Syrus

Chapter 7

Soon after gradation I packed up and went back home to Chicago. I was glad that I did not have to go back to the old neighborhood (Robert Taylor Homes). My family had moved away. They were now living in the Englewood area. This area was still low income, but after 22 years of the family being in the projects this was supposed to be better.

I began to work for the Chicago Transit Authority (CTA) as a part-time operator. My desire was to teach but I knew that I would have to start as a substitute teacher in order to do that. I also needed to figure out a way to raise money to go back to school to pursue my Master's degree. So I worked for CTA at night and pursued teaching during the day. Eventually, thanks to one of my former teachers

Dr. Thomas, I was accepted as a substitute teacher for the Chicago Public School (CPS).

Working those two jobs kept me on a tight schedule. Because I was part-time for CTA, my schedule was split. I would work mainly during the rush hours. Some days I would work from 6 AM until 9 AM and then be back from 3:30 PM until 6PM. This schedule did not allow me to accept many substitute teaching jobs, since school started before 9 AM.

I could not leave CTA, at least not yet. The money was good. Substitute teaching was a way to get into the door; however, it did not pay much. Yes, I had a desire to teach. Yes, I had a desire to give back to the community. But no, I was not going to put myself in the position of being financially strapped. The idea of being broke was scary and it was a place that I did not plan to return to. Knowing my psyche at the time, the temptation to return to some of my street resources, including selling drugs, would have been too great.

Having worked at CTA during my summers in college gave me an advantage over some of the other new hires. I was always ambitious and tried to display leadership potential in anything that I did, including driving a bus. I had an impeccable work ethic. I was always on time and tried to be available whenever I was needed. I would try to go out of my way to impress the bosses. That strategy paid off. In less than a year, I was promoted to a full time operator. This allowed me to have a straight night shift. I would be more available to accept teaching assignments during the day.

My school day would end about 2:45 PM. My shift at CTA started at 4 PM. I had just enough time to make it home, shower and be in uniform at the terminal in time for my shift. It was a tight schedule but it was what I chose to do. I had a goal and I was willing to sacrifice and do what was necessary to achieve it.

It wasn't always easy. Many times I would be tired and wonder if it was worth it. It would be those times that I would receive encouragement from images of the past.

My bus route included areas of my old neighborhood. I would often see some of the guys that I grew up with, many who would get on the bus surprised to see me behind the wheel.

"Lil Fella, is that you man? What sup?" It was one of the guys that I grew up with.

"Hey man. How are you doing", I said, as he got on the bus.

He sat near the front of the bus. We chatted for a few blocks.

"Man, you work for CTA? How did you get a gig like this? You need to hook a brother up.", he said enthusiastically.

Working for the CTA was seen as a high achievement in my community. It was seen as a stable, high paying job. It was an urban blue collar job that you could retire from comfortably. For many in my community, landing a job like this was the end of the goal, the crowning achievement. For me, it was simply a stepping stone.

"You need to go down there and apply. I don't know if they are hiring but it never hurts to see. Put your application in and see what happens. They will do a background check and call you in for drug testing." I told him.

"Aw man. That's messed up. See, I caught this case about a year ago... aw wow. And drug testing huh. So, do they test for just some drugs or all of them", he asked, rubbing his face.

"All of them", I laughed.

"Oh well...Hey this is my stop coming up. Hang tight brotha... it was good seeing you", he said as he stood up and walked to the door, holding the hand rails so he wouldn't fall.

"You too", I said as I pulled to the curb for the bus stop.

That could have been me. That could still be me, if I am not careful. You are doing the right thing. Stay focused. I thought to myself.

In order to stay focused, I would need to address my spirituality and not just deal with working and obtaining material things. During the summer before my junior year of college, I was licensed to preach the Gospel by Pastor Agee. However, when I returned from school and moved into the Englewood area, I felt led to explore other ministering options. My search led me to Bread of Life Missionary Baptist Church under the leadership of Pastor Johnson. It also helped that my lady friend, who later became my wife, went there also.

Pastor Johnson was doing something phenomenal in the Englewood area. Although this area was much better than the Robert Taylor Homes I grew up in, it was still an area marred with violence and economic hardship. Therefore, for a ministry to build a $4 million complex in this neighbor was tremendous. But, Pastor Johnson was a tremendous person.

Pastor Johnson had a heart for evangelism and I found that my passion was there also. I enjoyed going out to meet new people and introducing them to my faith and my church. Soon, I was appointed the head of the evangelism team. This was a wonderful experience and fed my need to exercise leadership. As a result of the efforts of many, including myself, the church grew.

I spoke with Pastor Johnson about becoming an ordained minister. I felt that God was leading me to this next step. I had a passion for evangelism and sharing the news about Christ. I realize that many people get a little nervous about evangelism and it produces pictures in many people's minds of pushy Christians hitting you with a bible screaming, "Do you know Jesus"? But true evangelism comes as you share your life and faith with those around you. If Dips had not shared with me his faith, I do not know where I would have ended up. At the rate I was going, prison or possibly death would have been my fate.

After sitting under the mentorship and training of Pastor Johnson for 3 years, it was finally time for my ordination. I was so excited. Although I was licensed to preach and had preached several times at other churches and even for Pastor Johnson, I was finally being ordained. I was no longer a "minister in training". I would be able to do a number of things including opening my own ministry.

Many of my friends were there, including many of the ministers that had allowed me to preach in their churches. Our ordination took place in an open assembly. There were 4 other candidates with me. Each of us was given a test of 35 questions. We would not be ordained if we did not pass with a score of 85% or higher. The test was not very difficult, but I studied anyway. I did not want nerves to get the best of me.

As were the rules for a Baptist ordination, if you were married, your wife had to be present. They wanted to make sure that you and your wife were in agreement and that you were a person of character. If your wife painted a dismal picture of your character, you would not be ordained.

As the ordination judges left the room to meet and decide who would be ordained, I sat near my wife. We were in agreement that this was the path that God had set before me. My wife had grown up in this church and loved the ministry very much. We knew in our spirits that this was the right thing to do.

The judges returned and announced their findings to the congregation. All 5 of us passed. We were ordained immediately.

The ordination was only a ceremony that acknowledged to the public the work that God had set before us in private. As we often say about baptism, it is an outward demonstration of an inward change. But these outward demonstrations can be powerful. Although I was committed to the work of the ministry that God had laid on my heart, this ordination service fueled a tremendous change in my heart and mind. I realized that I was no longer "Lil Fella", or "Larry", or even "Lawrence". I was now Rev. Lawrence Perkins. It was not just a name of respect, but also great responsibility. I prayed that God would make me worthy of the name.

*Goodness makes greatness truly valuable, and greatness
makes goodness much more serviceable.*

Matthew Henry

Chapter 8

After teaching several years as a substitute teacher, the opportunity to teach full time became available. This is what I wanted to do. This had been the goal. It was finally here.

I resigned from my position at the CTA and began working as an eighth grade teacher in the Back of the Yards community. I taught science and social studies.

I was so excited about the opportunity to really give back to the community. To be able to teach 8th graders was a dream come true. I wanted to be able to make a difference in the lives of young people, just as Mr. Richardson and so many others had made in my life.

I also knew the importance of the eighth grade. This was the year that determined whether or not a young person would go to high school and what options would be available to them once they were there. The study habits and discipline that they would develop this year would make a difference in the rest of their lives. If I could get them interested in school, particularly science, I would help them create a better path for themselves. If I was a bad teacher and showed little care and compassion for these students, I could lose them. The challenge was exhilarating.

I decided that I needed to increase my level of commitment to the students at the school. The afterschool program was looking for a basketball coach. Being the sports enthusiast that I am, this was a natural fit. Afterschool programs provide a safe haven and an alternative to drugs and gangs. Team sports, such as basketball, also help students develop a sense of character and teamwork.

One Monday in particular, I remember having a good basketball practice with my team. We were a close knit team and everyone got along with each other very well. We were preparing for a big game and we felt good about our chances. After practice several of the students gave me a high five, which was our standard ritual.

Getting home that evening, I turned the television on. As I walked away, I caught a glimpse of two familiar faces on the screen. I looked back and thought to myself, *That looks like Davon and Robert.* I looked at the banner running below the picture. It read "Two students killed by gang violence".

I could hardly breathe. I felt a knot in my stomach that was so tense I felt has if I would pass out. "No!" I screamed. "Not my students".

It took a few minutes for it to become real to me. Those young men were not just my students; they were also on the basketball team. I had just shared a high five with them hours earlier. They told me they were on their way home.

But they never made it home. They were gunned down by a 12 year old that wanted to join a gang. His initiation was to kill two people. For him, killing 2 people that were not part of a gang would be good since he would not have to worry about gang retaliation. Davon and Robert just happened to be near.

I could not sleep that night. I was a role model to these two boys and a father figure like Mr. Richardson was to me. I wondered what I could have done differently. Did I miss something? Should I have driven them home? Was God trying to tell me that something was going to happen and I missed it?

I also wondered what I would tell the rest of my class. What could I say to the other 26 students in my class? What answers could I give them? I was struggling to find the answers myself. How could I explain to them that even if they stay away from drugs, go to school and stay away from the gangs that this, too, could be their fate? I stayed up all night long pondering the answers and crying out to God to help me.

All morning as I prepared for school, I tried to stay focused. *I must be strong for the kids. Lord help me.* As I reached the school and got out of my car, my students rushed the car. One student cried, "What are we going to do now? They died for no reason." Another student said, "We were just hanging out having fun, a boy came up to them and shot one of them in the head and the other one in the back". She still had on the bloody shirt from the night before.

I reached out and hugged the student. Other students joined in and it turned into a group hug. "It's going to be alright", I said. "We will get through this. We will talk in class".

I gently broke away from the group. Struggling to hold back my own tears, I walked into the building, towards my classroom. I could hear the voices of several of my colleagues saying, "Stay focused". I nodded and continued to look down on the floor as I walked. I could not make eye contact with anyone. If I did, I knew the flood gates would open.

Once I reached the classroom, I had a chance to look at the desks where these two young students sat next to each other. I noticed that one student left his home work on the desk. *I got to move these desks. The others kids will crack if they have to see these desks.*

As I moved Davon and Robert's desks out of the room, a note fell out of one of the desk. It stated, "When I grow up what I want to be..." It was not completed. It would never be completed. I took a deep breath and said a little prayer.

The bell rang. All 26 eighth grade students came to school that day. No one was absent or tardy. Many came crying and some were wearing the same clothes that they had on the night before with blood stains on them. When the students came in the class, they looked at the area where the students once sat in classroom. I was so glad that I moved those desks.

There was complete silence for an hour in the classroom until the crisis counselors came. There was much to say but little energy to say it. How can you reach and teach students when they have just witnessed two of their classmates gunned down right before their very eyes? Unfortunately, this was not a rare occurrence in many urban areas particularly Chicago. It seemed at least once a month, if not more, some classroom, some teacher, some classmates were feeling this same loss. We often see on the news where some young person was killed. We may not know them, but someone does. They had to deal with the pain and in some way find out how to go on with their lives. We had to do the same.

It is incumbent upon us to understand our greatness and believe in it so that we do not cheapen and profane ourselves.

Meir Kahane

Chapter 9

I spent four years teaching at Richard J. Daley Elementary school. Shortly after that, an opportunity came for me to teach at Beethoven Academic Center. This was the school that I attended as a child and subsequently graduated from the 8th grade.

The school was now under the leadership of Frances Oden. Mrs. Oden was my 5th grade teacher during my time at the school. I was so happy to be back in my old neighborhood, really giving back to my community.

It was very surreal. Working back in the community allowed me to see old friends. I was actually teaching their children and grandchildren. I was also able to see the old

Robert Taylor Housing projects being demolished. There had been talk about relocating the families and tearing this complex down for years but many thought it would never happen. There would be so many families to relocate.

At one time, the Robert Taylor Homes was the largest housing project in the world. It was composed of 28 sixteen story high-rise buildings, mostly arranged in U-shaped clusters of three, stretching for two miles. It was completed in 1962 and named for Robert Rochon Taylor, the son of the first African-American architect accredited in the United States. Taylor was the first African American to be chairman of the Chicago Housing Authority. He was an advocate for scattering low income housing throughout the city and strongly opposed the city of Chicago's plan to limit black occupancy in public housing to predominantly black neighborhoods. He resigned his position when it became evident that the city would continue with a policy of racial segregation. Two years after he died, this huge housing project was initiated. Ironically, it was named in honor of him. If he were alive at the time, he probably would not only have protested the naming of the project, but the actual building of the complex.

The Beethoven Academic Center had changed so much over the years. There were, of course, some physical changes. However, there were other changes. There was a loving staff and excellent leadership under Mrs. Oden and then under Mrs. Stewart, once Mrs. Oden retired.

I was assigned to the room which was the same room I was in when I was in the 8th grade. This was home. Here, I was able to really relate to the students, teachers and parents. I understood their struggles and I could relate to their fears. I felt that I was really able to make a difference in the lives of these young people. I was often told that I did. I would like to believe I did.

During this time I was given the opportunity to speak at my alma mater, DuSable High School for their 2004 Commencement Exercise along with Rev. Jessie Jackson Sr., President and Founder of the Rainbow Push Coalition. It was truly an honor. I had seen him on television so many times but to have the opportunity to meet him was extraordinary. Rev. Jackson congratulated me on a "job well done".

During my speech, I thanked several of the people who made a difference in my life, including Mr. Richardson and Dr. Hamberlin. Dr. Hamberlin was a science teacher and the founder of Sophisticated Gents, a boy's social club at the school. Dr. Hamberlin taught for 40 years at DuSable High School and was a nationally recognized teacher.

I admired Dr. Hamberlin. He taught me how to dress, conduct and carry myself as a young man in the community. Dr. Hamberlin encouraged me to attend his former school, Alcorn State University.

Difficulty, my brethren, is the nurse of greatness - a harsh nurse, who roughly rocks her foster - children into strength and athletic proportion.

William C. Bryant

Chapter 10

Life was good. I felt accomplished. I was proud of myself and could finally see a good future. Before I could get used to the possibility of really experiencing the good life, it seemed all hell broke loose. Things began to deviate from the plans I had made for myself. My whole life began to take a downward spiral all at once.

The death of a loved one or friend alters the lives of those left behind, sometimes in a drastic way. Imagine two family members passing, one right after the other. Whether you are strong enough to withstand it determines how you are able to move on without that person. My family had to visit the funeral home more times than most people. In the month of April, my sister Brenda died. The next month my grandfather Jack Perkins died.

My sorrows still didn't end after their deaths. Neither of them was sick enough for us to expect them to die, they just did. To add more stress to this situation, both my mother and father were admitted to Holy Cross hospital at the same time. Both of them always had health issues. However, they seemed to get worse because of the death of my sister and grandfather only two months earlier. The things I thought about most were, when would this pain end and how the family would make it through this? Would we visit that funeral home again? I hoped we wouldn't.

After a few days of visiting my parents in the hospital, we finally got a report from the doctor. He discussed health issues for both my mom and dad. One of them would need more urgent care at this point. We learned a few days later that my mom would be coming home soon, but as for my dad, the news was not as comforting. My mother's health continued to get better and in a short amount of time she was released. My father, on the other hand, was another story.

I was accustomed to seeing my father as I have always remembered him. He was of average height, very handsome, hardworking, loving and kind. Although this was my mother's second marriage, he was the love of her life. They had two children together, my sister and me. My other 9 sisters and brothers were born from her first union. My father loved and took care of all 11 children, treating all of us the same. He was a strong man of honor, one who valued the idea of family.

The next few days and weeks would become some of the most difficult times of my life. My father, Lawrence Perkins Sr. was struggling everyday to hold on to his life. My father was addicted to alcohol. Almost every day of his adult life he enjoyed a drink of Peppermint Snap or had a bottle of Wild Irish Rose Wine. This everyday drinking took a big toll on his body. None of us ever thought what the effects of his drinking everyday would do to his liver. I always thought that liver damage generally came from drinking hard alcohol. I thought my father was safe. Later I learned that a person could drink enough wine to destroy their liver over the years. We didn't think about the amount of damage that had been done.

The doctors were doing tests to pin point what was going on with him. We were not naive to the point that there were major health problems for him to overcome. We just didn't know what they were. I remember the doctor saying words like diabetes, insulin, and blood testing. My father did not have diabetes to my knowledge but symptoms associated with it were the ones my father had been experiencing probably longer than any of us knew. The symptoms that brought him to the hospital this time were weakness, fatigue, loss of appetite, nausea, vomiting, weight loss, abdominal pain and bloating.

My father always looked healthy until the final symptoms became very obvious. His abdomen was extremely large. He reminded me of how a woman looks at the end of her pregnancy. This is when we learned that he had been diagnosed with cirrhosis of the liver 2 months earlier. He had not shared this with us. We were totally shocked, sad and unprepared.

The doctors at Holy Cross Hospital told us that they would do everything possible to make him comfortable. I didn't think at the time what that meant. Almost a week later my father was transferred to hospice care. Just the thought of my dad being labeled as one of those people whom the doctors said there was nothing else they could do made me extremely sad. They told us that all they could do at this point was to make him comfortable. I knew then that he would not get better. The thought of my father being terminally ill scared me.

I wanted to mentally store all of my memories about my dad right away. I figured that my memories would soon hide in the back part of my mind, becoming distant after a while. I needed to do whatever it took to keep those memories fresh. I began to flash back to my earlier thoughts and conversations with my father. He often told me that he had always worked a job from the time he was a young man. He grew up in Chicago, in the Chatham neighborhood on the Southside. He had been employed for 35 years at Marcus Brush Company as a manager in the shipping department.

I was proud that he was, and had always been faithful to working and supporting his family all of his life. He always told me that he didn't make much money, but every dime he earned went to support his wife and children. He was saddened by the fact that he worked sun up to sun down and still couldn't make ends meet. We still had to depend on the government and other charitable agencies to get by.

I remember going to Operation Push to get free food baskets along with hundreds of other people. We stood in line for hours. It was worse in the winter time. I shiver even now just thinking of how cold it was waiting in subzero weather, trying to be patient. After all, we needed food to eat. They gave out baskets once each month. We would see the same people every month. We had it down to a routine. If you could patiently wait, you would go home with enough food to feed the family at least 2 meals. The food they gave you went along with whatever you had at home. They didn't give out meat, but they did give you a large block of cheese.

That government cheese made the best grilled cheese sandwiches I had ever tasted. I ate plenty of them when I was younger. My stomach was always filled with whatever we had in the refrigerator. I could not be choosey. I wanted to be full.

We visited my dad in hospice for about 3 weeks. It did not seem that he was improving at all. He was conscious some days. I think he pretended to sleep because he didn't want to talk. That didn't stop me from going to see him every day.

I remember one day in particular I felt that I needed to go to the hospice right away. I did not know why I had this feeling of urgency. I would go every day. I mentioned this urgent feeling to my mother. She said the strangest thing to me, which I would never forget. She said, "This will be the day that he will die". When she said that, it was like someone kicked me in my stomach. Fear gripped me and I felt a little dizzy. I tried not to let my mother see my reaction. When I looked in her eyes, I could see an indescribable sadness. She looked serious and I knew she believed what she had just said to me.

To lighten the conversation, there was a mention of picking up Chinese food on the way home. I was glad to talk about something other than what my mom had just told me. I left her and went to the hospice. All the way there I thought about that eerie conversation. I tried to put it out of my mind because I was not ready for my dad to die.

I should have started preparing myself when I first heard what my mom said. As I was getting off of the elevator at the hospice, and walking towards my dad's room, I could hear the nurse saying over and over, "Mr. Perkins, Mr. Perkins can you hear me?" I did not hear my father respond. I stepped into the room quickly going straight to the bed where my father was laying. The nurse said to him, "Mr. Perkins, your son is here to see you, can you hear me?" My father never said anything, although I did see that he was conscious. He reached out his hand. I held his hand and locked eyes with him. For just for a second, I blinked. In that second, in that moment, he passed. I could feel the release in my hand. His breath stopped and he was gone.

I took a few minutes to get myself together. What should I do first? I knew I needed to call home. I was nervous, how do I tell a woman who had been married to this man for 45 years that he had just passed away? Although she knew in her heart that today was the day, I did not want to be the one to confirm this. However, it had to be done. I had no plan as to how I would tell her. I picked up the telephone at my dad's bedside and dialed our home phone number. I was not ready to tell anyone who answered the phone what had just happened. When I heard the voice on the phone, I realized it was my aunt Jean. I was relieved that she was there with my mom to give her the bad news. I didn't have the courage or strength to tell my mother, so my aunt delivered the bad news. This would be the third trip to the funeral home in a little over three months. I called my pastor.

The service was held at the Bread of Life Church on the Southside of Chicago, in the Englewood neighborhood. My family members and I walked around in a daze for the next two weeks or so. I was in mourning and my heart was flooded with sadness and disbelief. At some time during the planning of the funeral service I was told that I was expected to do the eulogy. This blew my mind. Why did they think I was strong enough to stand before people and talk about my father in the past tense?

I began to write down the thoughts I wanted to share at the service. My father was a good man. He had his issues and he was not perfect, but he was a good man. I thought about how blessed I was to have a father in my life. Even though growing up I did not appreciate it. I often used the excuse that he wasn't there enough for me and that contributed to my gang involvement. But as I sat there, preparing my thoughts, I realized that it was an excuse. My father, as well as my mother did the best they could do; the best they knew how to do.

The service was very emotional. There was lots of crying, some loud and some soft murmurs. When my time to speak came I got out of my seat and walked to the podium. I found it very difficult to even look at the casket knowing that my father laid there stiff and straight. I turned my head and walked up the stairs to deliver these last words of kindness to him.

I didn't think I would make it through to the end of the eulogy. I did. As the family lined up to leave the church for the cemetery, I glanced at my mother's face. I knew right then her life would never be the same, neither would mine.

Nothing liberates our greatness like the desire to help, the desire to serve.

Marianne Williamson

Chapter 11

At this stage of my life, I had accomplished several goals. That felt good to me. To reach the next level of accomplishments meant I would have to make some career changes. This would include leaving my current position at Beethoven Elementary School. I had taken my educational skills back to my old neighborhood, but now it was time to move on. It was important to give back to my old community and I felt that I had made a difference in the lives of my friend's sisters and brothers.

My old friend's younger sisters and brothers knew me from my reputation as being a successful person who came back to the area after getting out of college. I was a constant reminder that with hard work and commitment you could be anything you wanted to be. Some, of course, heard the message and went on to accomplish their goals. Others didn't listen and as a result, they were swallowed up by the oppression that surrounded them. I felt that my impact was successful, so I didn't feel bad moving on.

I had always had a desire to work in a leadership capacity even when I was a young man. I knew that I wanted to affect the lives of other people in a greater way. My passion had led me to the field of education. However, I felt that I could do a greater work in this area. In order to accomplish this, I would need to address my own education. I would need to return to school. Although I had a B.A. degree, I would need at least a Masters in Education to pursue leadership opportunities in this field. My greatest desire was to help other young people realize their goals. I enrolled at National Louis University located in downtown Chicago pursuing a Masters in Education and Leadership.

It would take almost 2 years to complete this program. While still in school, I became more aware of the success that charter schools were having, particularly among minority students. Charter schools operate as independent public schools. The fundamental principles of these schools include choice, accountability and autonomy. Parents may choose to send their children to charter schools. Students are not required to attend based on residential requirements. Teachers can also choose to work at a particular charter school and not be assigned to a school based on seniority or other factors.

Charter schools also operate under a certain level of autonomy. Although charter schools must adhere to many of the laws and regulations as public schools, they are freed from some of the red tape that plagues public schools. However, charter schools are accountable for the performance of their students and are held to rigorous fiscal and management standards. If a charter school does not meet its standards, that school will be closed.

Although the idea of charter schools had been around since the late 1980's, Minnesota was the first state to pass actual charter school laws in 1991. In 1996, Illinois passed its charter school law which allowed 15 charter schools to open in Chicago.

The charter school educational model impressed me. As an educator, I was particularly impressed with the idea of autonomy. I wanted to be able to spend more time educating my students as opposed to extraneous and what I often felt was unnecessary paperwork. I was also intrigued by the idea of true accountability. A number of my teaching colleagues were dedicated teachers that truly wanted what was best for the student. However, as a student of the public schools and as a teacher, I saw too many teaching professionals that just did not care about the quality of service that they provided to their students. More blame was placed on the child that did not learn as opposed to the teacher that did not teach. I was excited that these new schools were available and I sought an opportunity to become part of this exciting shift in education.

After researching several options, in 2005 I decided to place my resume for consideration at the United Neighborhood Organizations (UNO). At that time UNO successfully managed several charter schools in Chicago, serving primarily the Hispanic community. UNO began in 1984 as a grass root community organization building leadership within Chicago's Hispanic neighborhoods. Their mission was to address local issues such as street violence and an educational system that did not meet the needs of its community. UNO became a major voice in the Chicago's school reform movement and eventually went on to establishment of the UNO Charter School Network in 2004.

I was hired by UNO as the Dean of Students for Octavio Paz School. Octavio Paz was UNO's first charter school. This school was failing until UNO assumed full responsibility and took over the day to day operations in 2000. In three short years, Octavio Paz had reversed its declining test scores and began achieving some of the highest test scores among charter schools in Chicago.

I was honored to accept this offer which allowed me to work directly with these students on a daily basis. My responsibilities included student attendance, ensuring school safety and supporting the teaching staff. I also served as a sounding board for many of the students. This position gave me an opportunity to help shape the future of these students in the same way that Mr. Richardson and Dr. Hamberlin did for countless students at DuSable. I was excited for this chance to help make a difference in their lives.

I was also able to complete my Master's Degree in Education during this time. This was such an accomplishment for me. Not only was I the first from my family to go to college, I had now received my Master's. I was able to stay focused on my goals and as a result I had triumphed over the obstacles that desired to keep me down. I felt extremely blessed.

Around the second year of working at UNO I received a telephone call from the CEO of UNO with an opportunity to relocate to New Orleans to help start a new charter school after the damage of Hurricane Katrina. As most people, I watched the destruction and devastation of Hurricane Katrina. My heart ached for the people, particularly the children. I loved taking on new challenges, so I agreed to travel to New Orleans. I took a weekend and went to see the area that I would possibly be working in.

Before Hurricane Katrina, the name "New Orleans" provoked visions of fun. The "Big Easy" was known for great music, great food and the largest citywide party, the Mardi Gras, that one could imagine. I had always wanted to visit the French Quarter, Bourbon Street and some of the great jazz and blues clubs that New Orleans was famous for.

I arrived in New Orleans and headed for my hotel before going to see the school building. Although the hurricane was more than 2 years prior, you could see that even areas in downtown New Orleans had not fully recovered. One thing I noticed upon arriving at the hotel was that there were blacks working at the front desk. It dawned on me that I had never seen blacks working the front desk at a major hotel. On television programs and commercials, these positions where always portrayed by other actors. The truth was that my travels had been pretty much limited to Chicago and my college town of Lorman,

Mississippi. Although I now had a Master's in Education, I realized that there was so much more for me to learn.

After I got checked in and unpacked, I was taken on a quick tour of the city. The city looked like a beautiful jewel that had been extremely battered and bruised. You could tell that underneath the scars was a precious gem waiting to recover and unfold. Many of the businesses in the downtown areas had reopened although you could see abandoned shops and stores intermingled in. Watermarks remained on many buildings showing how the flood waters rose to the second floor of many structures.

As we drove away from the center of the city, the remnants of the disaster were more prevalent. As we approached the New Orleans' ninth ward, my heart sank. As most people, I had seen the devastation on television during the weeks and months after Katrina. I had even seen an update on the area that was aired a year or so after Katrina. But this was two years later.

What I saw was unbelievable. There were blocks after blocks of homes that had been destroyed by the floods. Some homes had been torn down but many remained standing. I saw houses where the roof and walls had collapsed and nothing remained other than the frame.

Although you could see that the cleanup effort was tremendous, there was still a lot of work to be done.

We arrived at the building that would house the school UNO wanted to open. You could still see the watermarks from the ravaging flood waters. As we walked up the path to the building, we noticed that the second and third floors looked okay, but the first floor really would need a lot of work. As we accessed the property, we realized that there would be a lot of work to do, but it was not impossible.

As we headed back to the car, we noticed that we had drawn the attention of some of the local residents. A young man came up to us. I quickly held out my hand and greeted him. He told us that this was his school before the storm hit. He reminisced about an assignment that was due on the day the storm hit that he was unable to turn in. One day you are a student, going to school, hanging out with your friends, complaining about teachers and the next day your life has totally changed.

"Are you here to fix my school, open it up so that I can go back?" he asked. Before I knew it, my reply flew out of my month, "Yes, yes we will". Although I had not decided before coming to New Orleans if I would even take the position, I felt a sense of destiny in the answer I gave him. I knew that this was part of the plan that God had for me. I knew this was where I was needed. This one child, and the hundreds of others like him, was a major reason I decided that I would return to New Orleans to work for the next 2 years.

As I flew back to Chicago, I thought about my pending decision. I had not officially accepted the position but I knew that I would. However, there were some major issues that I had to address. How would I tell my mother? She had been ill off and on, particularly since my father passed. I did not want be that far away from her. I knew that I would have to depend on other family members to watch out for her. I needed some reassurance that she would be okay, and that someone would be there with her. We were able to get the help that we needed. So I was off to New Orleans, a few days later.

The news about UNO's plans to help in New Orleans made the local Chicago newspapers. On the day I left, the Chicago Sun-Times sent a reporter to talk to me about the upcoming project. I was elated and honored to share a full page story about my participation and plans for New Orleans.

I was one of three employees to relocate from the Chicago area from UNO to start the Esperanza Charter School. Esperanza, which is the Spanish word for hope, had nearly 300 students enrolled, even before the doors opened. Many of the student population would be Hispanic immigrants who had recently moved to New Orleans to help rebuild the city. Since many of these students did not speak English, it was difficult to integrate them in the current school system, which was already coping with major rebuilding challenges. Many of the New Orleans teachers relocated as a result of the Hurricane and decided not to return.

The school opening was successful. The students found a school that was full of love and support. I was expecting to have a number of behavior issues since many of these students lost so much in the hurricane, including family and loved ones. Many of the other students were children of immigrant workers. They were in a new country that was demanding them to learn a new language. I was pleasantly surprised to find very few behavior issues. My biggest challenge was students chewing gum in class.

I remained in New Orleans for two years. During this time, we graduated the first 8th grade class for the new school. For many of the immigrants, these students were the first in their families to achieve even this level of education. These students were excited about the opportunity to further their education in high school and many aspired to attend college.

I was grateful for the opportunity to help these young people find direction in their lives. I learned that the need for guided, directed focus transcends racial, economic and ethnic barriers. The same mentorship and direction that touched children in Chicago also touched children in New Orleans. Whether these children spoke perfect English, broken English or no English at all, they all needed to hear encouragement that they were special and that they had the ability to achieve greatness.

Be not afraid of greatness: some are born great, some achieve greatness, and some have greatness thrust upon them.

William Shakespeare

Chapter 12

I realized at a young age that my life's purpose involved young people. That is where my passion is. I imagine that my call to serve young people stems from my youth. I know what it is like to not have those mentors in your life to help lead and guide you. But I also know what it is like when those people are there. I know how it feels to be hopeless and think that there is no way out and that this is as good as it gets. I also know what it is like to have people believe in you and instill hope in you to the point that you believe that there is nothing impossible for you to achieve. This is what I desire to share with every person, particularly young person that I meet.

In my career as a teacher, I was able to touch the lives of many. I tried to the best of my ability to instill a sense of hope into their lives. I wanted them to realize that they had great futures ahead of them, regardless of their present conditions. They could choose to make something out of their lives if they stayed focus.

However, I was never able to really express the true source of that hope in a school setting. Youth ministry allowed me to not only share hope with people but to share what I believe to be the source of that hope. Having great mentors that believe in you is wonderful and needed. However, you need to have an inner, spiritual source of strength and determination. I believe that comes from knowing who you are in Jesus Christ.

My opportunity to share this spiritual message with young people on a consistent basis came when I answered an ad for a Youth Pastor in 2005. The church, Greater St. John Bible Church was a growing ministry located in Chicago's Austin community. Pastor Ira Acree also had a great passion for young people. We connected well and I was hired as the Children's Pastor.

My responsibilities included the children's church, nursery, children's choir and praise dancers. I worked with an awesome staff of 10 people to serve about 250 children every week.

Even with this, I sensed that there was a greater calling on my life. I would often dream of standing before thousands of people, preaching the Gospel of Jesus Christ and winning souls for the kingdom. After the sermon, people would flock to me saying how inspired they were and their desire to sow into the ministry to spread the word. They would also call me "Pastor" Perkins as opposed to "Reverend".

At first I thought that the dream was just that, a dream. But then the thoughts and desire to Pastor became greater and greater. The dream would become more frequent also. I began to see people differently, as if I were looking through a lense of compassion. I was developing what I later found out to be a Pastor's heart.

While I had worked with ministries for years as an ordained minister, I knew that being a Pastor was not something to be taken lightly. Of course, you needed to be called by God but that was subjective. If you were to ask most Pastors if they were called by God, the majority would say yes. Although many people judge Pastors from the outside and say that many are in it for the possible money and power it could bring, most Pastors would not agree. Being a Pastor is hard work, especially if done properly. You are looked up to as a father, teacher, mentor, counselor, career advisor, medical consultant, financial planner and community leader, among other things. If you make a mistake, particularly a moral one, you are deemed as "not saved". If you ever get sick with something beyond a cold, you are deemed as having little faith. God forbid that you face a divorce, have a child that is a cut-up in school, or make a bad business decision. No, being a Pastor is not an easy decision to make, even if you felt led by God to do it.

After what is known as "running from the call", I accepted that this was what God wanted me to do. It also helped that there were several ministers in my family, including my aunt Jean who was a pastor. While attending her church, Willing Workers, I received a prophetic message from my aunt Georgia, who is also a minister, that it was now time for me to stop running. It was time to deal with the call on my life to Pastor. My aunt, Pastor Jean Conley, agreed.

On February 7, 2010, I began New Anointing Ministries with 8 people. Our congregation grew quickly to over 40 people in a little over 2 months. We began looking for a facility to hold our services. We looked at several, but none seemed to be right for us.

My aunt Georgia invited me to speak at her home church, Redeeming's World Church of Hammond. I was familiar with Redeeming since many of my family members went there when I was younger. It was previously located in Chicago under the name of Redeeming Church of Christ. The current Pastor, Rev Paul A. Southerland, moved the church and its Christian school to Hammond, IN.

As I prepared for my message, I felt led by God to purchase a telescope. Since I minister a lot to children, I had become very illustrative in my preaching style. I feel that it is very important that the congregation see and visualize what you are saying. Using props can help.

At the end of my message, I began to speak a prophetic word to Pastor Southerland. I told him that the best was yet to come. The ministry was in a rebuilding phase. I spoke of all of the new people that God would be sending their way. As I looked in the telescope to dramatize this statement, I saw myself as one of the new people coming to the ministry. Before I knew it, I said that I see myself there in Hammond, building the kingdom.

As a preacher, it is easy to get caught up in the excitement of the presentation of the message. As we "flow in the anointing", we can boldly speak what we believe God has inspired us to say. However, once we have left the platform, and that rush is no longer there, we can sometimes question what we said.

After thinking about the powerful message I had delivered at Redeeming, I spent the next few days in prayer, confused by parts of the message. Hammond? *Why would I go to Hammond, Indiana,* I thought to myself. This was just a speaking engagement. I have a ministry. I am on staff at another one. Why would I see myself in Hammond?

Don't get me wrong. There were a lot of wonderful things in Hammond. I just did not understand at that moment what they had to do with me. Pastor Southerland is a seasoned and gifted Pastor also with a heart for youth. The ministry had a Christian school and childcare, the Hazel Young Academy, which was in its 10th year of operation. The campus was beautiful, located on Hohman Ave, with classrooms, gym, full commercial kitchen and sanctuary. Both the church and the school were rebuilding.

After several days of prayer, I believe I heard the answer to my question. The ministry I had started was actually to be a team to go Hammond. What? All of this time I thought I was building up my church, my ministry. I could quickly hear the correction in my spirit. It wasn't my ministry, it was God's ministry. I was his servant, not the other way around. I quickly accepted the new assignment. My team quickly integrated with the ministry and we are working towards expanding the ministry through kingdom building classes, community outreach and evangelism and expanded youth ministries.

An ignorance of means may minister to greatness, but an ignorance of aims make it impossible to be great at all.

Elizabeth Barrett Browning

Chapter 13

There are several things that I want you to walk away with after reading this book.

When you are determined to succeed, you can let no one or nothing hamper you from achieving your goals. There is no room for excuses or blaming someone else. You may have had a rough childhood, you may have been hit with some type of horrible disease, or you may have undergone some tremendous abuse. Whatever challenges you may face, you must know that you can overcome them. You were created with the power to achieve. Learn how to tap into that power.

Spiritual growth is crucial. While it is not the intent of this book to convert anyone to a particular religious world view, it is important to convey the belief that one must address every aspect of themselves, including their spirituality in order to fully mature. Without it, you will find yourself attempting to fill a spiritual void with material things. It will not work.

I quickly found in my life that mentorship is the key to excellence. Most people seek to learn from others. Most people have a desire to share what they know. If these desires are not guided in the proper way, disastrous results can occur. My desire to learn from others initially resulted in gang activity. It was here that I was first mentored. It was here that other people took me under their wings to share with me what they knew. Unfortunately, drugs, violence and sex were all they knew. Although I was on my way to becoming an "excellent" gang member, that route would have, without doubt, led to my destruction.

I also found that peer pressure was a smoke screen designed to deceive those that look through it. Everyone is not doing it. Whatever your "it" is that you feel you must do in order to be cool is not happening everywhere. Every cool teenager is not having sex. Everyone is not trying drugs. Everyone does not take a drink every once in a while. Don't believe the hype. It is simply not happening that way. The deception of peer pressure can lead to destructive behavior.

I was blessed to encounter the right type of mentors before my destruction took place. Without the mentorship of Mr. Richardson, Dr. Hamberlin, Dr. Thomas, Pastor Agee and many others, there is no doubt in my mind that I would have ended up in prison, if I was lucky but most probably dead. These gentlemen went out of their way to help not only me, but countless others. However, there are not enough of them to go around.

We must have more mentors in our communities that will actively reach out to our young people. This is not a race, gender or economic status issue. All of our young people need mentors that will help them as they are on the path of self discovery. Parents cannot do it alone. It really does take a village to raise a child and it is time for the village to step up and take action.

However, the village is not a replacement for strong family involvement. Parents must put their children as a priority in their lives. Not just providing for the children but the actual nurture of the children. There must be quality family time that is not substituted with gadgets or other material things. We must take time to listen to our children and be the parent, not just the friend they need.

Perhaps the most important lesson here is to believe in yourself and do not be afraid to believe in others. You can have a perfect family, wonderful mentors, and a strong spiritual foundation. However, if you do not believe in yourself, none of those things will sustain you. You will see parental involvement as "nagging parents". You will see wonderful mentors as "noisy teachers". You will see a strong spiritual foundation through the eyes of a person that has been called to "suffer many things", serving a God who can do great things, but never experiencing those things in your life.

Finally, stay focused. You have been designed to achieve awesome things. Every resource that you need in order to succeed has already been created. Commit to your mental and spiritual growth. Find the right mentors to help guide you to your destiny. Believe in all that you have been created to be.

As my journey continues, I am forever grateful to the men and women who have inspired me to believe that I could achieve greatness. The same is true for you. No matter where you are in your life you can still achieve greatness. As William Arthur Ward so eloquently stated, "Greatness is not found in possessions, power, position, or prestige. It is discovered in goodness, humility, service, and character." Regardless of the boundaries or limitations set before you, strive to simply do good things, have a humble heart, service your fellow man and have impeccable character. Allow your greatness to transcend all boundaries.

8620714R0

Made in the USA
Lexington, KY
16 February 2011